W9-DEX-529

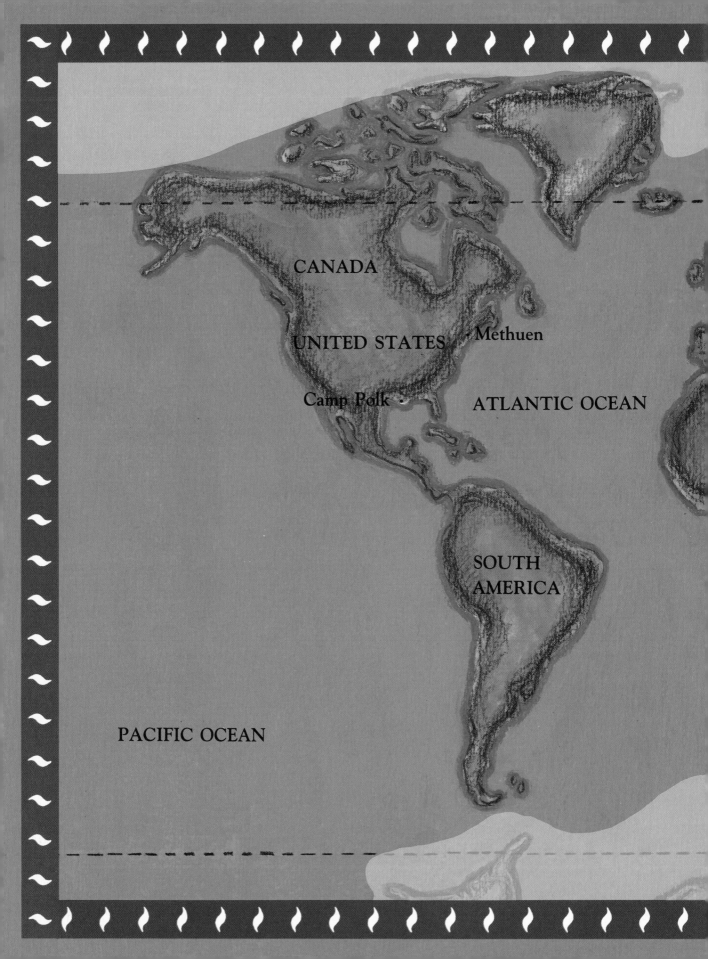

For Sarah, Joshua,
Abaigeal, and Hannah.
—R.C.

Front cover photograph copyright © 1993 Capital Cities/ABC, Inc.
Back cover photograph from the Roger Caras Library.

Photo Credits:
Pages 6, 10, 11, 15, 18, 19, 26, 27 (top), 32, 34, 35, 37 (top), 40, 45, from the Roger Caras library; Page 8,
© 1993 Capital Cities/ABC, Inc; Page 9 (top and bottom), © Dave McMichael; Pages 12, 14, 16,
17, 29, © Frederick D. Atwood; Page 13 (top), courtesy Methuen Historical Commission; Page 13 (bottom),
© W. Perry Conway; Pages 20, 22, 23, 24, 25, 30, 31, © Wolfgang Kaehler; Page 27 (bottom), © Mauritius
GMBH/Phototake NYC; Page 28, © Mark Newman/Phototake NYC; Page 33, © Erwin and Peggy Bauer;
Page 36 , © Eugene Underwood, Jr; Pages 37 (bottom), 38, © ASPCA; Page 39, © Ivan Tors.

Logo design by Stephen Brenninkmeyer
Jacket and book design by Alex Jay/Studio J
Map by Nin Chi

Special thanks to Kristen Breck,
Gillian Bucky, and Jill Brubaker

Editor: Kathy Huck
Editorial Assistant: Vicky Rauhoufer

Library of Congress Cataloging-in-Publication Data

Caras, Roger A.
A world full of animals : the Roger Caras story / by Roger Caras.
p.   cm.—(The Great naturalists)
Includes index.
ISBN 0-8118-0654-5 : —ISBN 0-8118-0682-0 (pbk.)
1. Caras, Roger A. 2. Journalists—United States—Biography—Juvenile literature. 3. Naturalists—
United States—Biography—Juvenile literature. 4. Environmentalists—United States—Biography—
Juvenile literature. 5. Animals—Juvenile literature. [1. Caras, Roger A. 2. Environmentalists. 3.
Naturalists. 4. Animals.] I. Title. II. Series.
PN4874.C252A3 1994
508'.092—dc20
[B]   93-31009
CIP
AC

Distributed in Canada by Raincoast Books
112 East Third Avenue, Vancouver, B.C. V5T 1C8

10 9 8 7 6 5 4 3 2 1

Chronicle Books

A World Full of Animals
The Roger Caras Story

◆

A Byron Preiss Book

◆

by Roger Caras

Chronicle Books • San Francisco

TABLE OF CONTENTS

Introduction.................................8

A Country Childhood.................10

A Snake Lesson........................14

Penguins: The Tip of the Iceberg...........18

Africa: My Dream Come True..............26

The Royal Tusker of Sri Lanka...............32

Saving the Animals.......................36

Afterword...............................40

Organizations...........................42

Glossary................................43

Index...................................44

Introduction

A tiger shows affection for Roger on the Dick Cavett show, 1970.

Ever since I was a child, I have loved animals. I spent my childhood reading about them or observing them in my backyard. What started as a hobby became my job when I grew up. I am what you call a naturalist—a person who devotes his or her life to the study of animals and the natural world. You are probably familiar with the type of naturalist who conducts scientific studies of animals or the environment. But photographers, writers, and journalists, like myself, can be naturalists, too. I have tried to learn about animals and their habitats, and to share that knowledge with others. Television, film, and newspapers can reach millions of people—that's quite an audience!

Throughout my career as a naturalist, I have informed people about the dangers facing animals and our environment. When I joined ABC News in 1974, I was the only network correspondent assigned exclusively to covering animals and the environment. Since then I have delivered television's first report on the wild pandas of Szechwan, China, as well as stories on elephants in Sri Lanka, rhinoceroses in Africa, rattlesnakes in Texas, and moose in Maine. I have also covered environmental issues such as the disastrous 1988 *Exxon*

Valdez oil spill in Prince William Sound, Alaska.

Currently, as president of the American Society for the Prevention of Cruelty to Animals (ASPCA), I still inform people about the dangers facing our world's animals, but in different ways—by working to get laws passed that protect animals, and by creating programs that increase people's awareness of animal welfare. I also continue to work on projects for television, radio, magazines, and, of course, books. In addition, I continue to travel a lot. A typical year might include a trip to Africa, South or Central America, the Galápagos Islands, and an average of thirty states within the U.S. When I travel, I conduct research, meet with wildlife officials, and observe animals in their habitat. It's how I make my living. There is no rule that says work can't be fun.

My wife Jill and I now live in Maryland on a lovely old farm named Thistle Hill. We share our farm with eleven dogs, eight cats, four horses, two cows, a donkey, a llama, and two macaws. The two cows, Fat Susan Jane and Steakums, were rescued from cruel owners by humane workers and have come to our farm to live. Four of our dogs are greyhounds that were formerly used on dog racing tracks.

It would be impossible to write about all my experiences as a naturalist in one book, so I have put together my most memorable and fascinating moments. Animals have been the main characters in my life and are therefore the main characters in this book. After reading this, I hope you are encouraged to make animals a significant part of your life, too.

TOP: Roger and a few of his dogs at Thistle Hill.

BOTTOM: A llama, a donkey, and a horse share a home at Thistle Hill.

At an early age, Roger fell in love with animals. Five-year-old Roger (at right) sits atop a pony with his older brother, Sheldon.

A Country Childhood

I was born in 1928 in the small town of Methuen, thirty-five miles northwest of Boston. I was raised with my two brothers, Sheldon and Marshall. My mother, Bessie, was a bookkeeper and my father, Joseph, was an insurance man.

Methuen had open fields and meadows, streams and ponds, the lazy Spickett River, and dark, mysterious woodlands full of places to hide. With so much wild habitat there were, of course, wild animals. Round, fat muskrats lived in the river, and rabbits and meadow mice scurried across the fields. In the woods there were opossums, squirrels, skunks, deer, and raccoons.

There were also many kinds of birds: Baltimore orioles, bluebirds, blue jays, indigo buntings, goldfinches, cardinals, horned larks, hawks, owls, geese, ducks, and gulls. In the spring their songs were a nonstop musical performance.

Butterflies of all kinds also flitted in our gardens and in the meadows. There were other insects, too, like dragonflies, ladybugs, beetles, moths, flies, and, of course, mosquitoes, especially near the river and the ponds.

Like a lot of kids, my brothers and I always tried to keep pet snakes, frogs, turtles, and often baby birds that had been blown out of their nests. We were able to raise some of these animals and later turn them loose. Some died, though, no matter how hard we tried to save them, and we had a little plot for them in our garden that we surrounded with rocks. We always planted flowers around their graves. It became a special place for us.

When I was a baby, my family had a Boston terrier

As early as I can remember, I would venture into the meadows and woods to see animals. During my excursions, people would ask where I was going, and I would reply that I was traveling to China, to India, or to Africa. I didn't really know where those places were, but I knew I was going somewhere to discover the world of animals.

The Caras family in 1936. From left to right: Marshall (age 3), Bessie, Roger (age 8), Joseph, and Sheldon (age 12).

A young praying mantis.

When praying mantises first come out of their egg cases, or oothecae, *they are bright green, but as they grow, their colors dull. We used to pick them off leaves and branches hold them for a few minutes, and then let them go. I still like to do that today.*

named Bozo. When Bozo died, we got a collie we called Missy, and then a cocker spaniel we named Peter. Peter was my favorite. He had been hit by a car and broken his leg when he was young. The leg healed and he walked perfectly—unless he was being scolded. Then he limped. We also had a cat, a canary, and an aquarium full of bright gold-fish. I just couldn't imagine that there were people without pets. I couldn't understand how anyone could live without them.

Some kids in our town set traps for ani-mals, but most of us hated the idea. Occa-sionally we would find animals in the traps, and we would set them loose. One day when I was seven years old, I was walking in the woods. I smelled skunk, and then I saw a black-and-white animal caught in a trap. I just had to turn him loose, and I felt certain I could creep up on him and somehow get the jaws of that trap apart without being bitten, or worse yet, sprayed. I crept closer, keeping a careful eye on its every move. It was in pain, so I really can't blame it for what happened next. The skunk made his move—and I was the loser!

I ran home crying. My mother said she could smell me even before she heard my yowling. I was ordered to go out behind the house and strip off my clothes. My mother brought out a large washtub and had me sit in it while she poured can after can of tomato juice over me. My brother Sheldon then had to carry my clothes away on a stick and burn them.

After a half-hour soak in tomato juice I was ordered into another tub, this one full of very hot water. Then I really yowled. I thought they were trying to cook me! My mother lathered me with strong laundry soap and scrubbed me. Finally I was rinsed off, dried, and permitted to get into clean clothes. I have seen a lot of skunks since, but I have never put myself in a position to get sprayed again.

Spickett River, Methuen, Mass.

The Spickett River as it looked during Roger's childhood.

Even after my unfortunate encounter with the skunk, animals were to be my life's work and, outside of my family, my greatest joy. Methuen was a wonderful place to grow up—a place in which to learn and to explore. It was little wonder that growing up there gave me the idea that the world was full of animals.

A striped skunk.

A cottonmouth water moccasin.

A Snake Lesson

When I was almost twelve years old, my family moved to Boston. At this time I knew that I wanted to work with animals, so I started working at the Angell Memorial Animal Hospital. My first job at the hospital was cleaning animal cages. I then "moved up" to working in the laboratory where they put dogs and cats to sleep. Although this was necessary to ease an animal's suffering, I hated doing it and would lay awake each night apologizing to every dog and cat that was put to sleep. I only lasted several weeks because I couldn't bear to perform such a painful task.

At the age of fifteen, I started writing. I wrote mainly about animals, including my cocker spaniel, Peter. Some of my stories were published in my school literary magazine. In addition to writing, I also read a lot. My favorite book was *The Voyage of the Beagle*, which is about the naturalist Charles Darwin, and his trip around the world, observing plant and animal life. I read that book over and over, and I then decided what I was going to do: I, too, was going to travel around the world to see animals.

When I finished high school, I joined the army. The army started me on my travels. For training, I was sent to Louisiana, to a base then known as Camp Polk. The area around camp couldn't have been more different from Massachusetts. The woods were largely pine, and there were huge swamps. That was where I saw my first armadillos—wonderful, burrowing animals that looked

While in the army, Roger spent his spare time watching animals at zoos.

The cottonmouth water moccasin can have a deadly bite.

The thick-bodied cottonmouth snake spends most of its time in or near water. It is active at night, when it searches for food such as fish, amphibians, birds, and other snakes.

as if they were wearing armor. There were also huge wild pigs, some of which grew to weigh half a ton—about the weight of a motorcycle! There were plenty of deer and squirrels, and once on a hike I saw a black bear. But the animals I remember most from Camp Polk were the snakes. There seemed to be no end to them, and many of them were quite dangerous.

I quickly made friends with another trainee named Bill Pryor. Bill and I asked the camp's doctor if he would like a display of the dangerous snakes, spiders, and insects found in the camp so that the other soldiers, particularly those who had grown up in cities, would know what to avoid. The doctor was pleased with the idea.

Bill and I caught a copperhead snake, a pygmy rattlesnake, a coral snake, a cottonmouth water moccasin, and a timber rattlesnake. That rattlesnake seemed to live for the day when it could get even with us for capturing it. It was always alert and on guard. But it was the cottonmouth water moccasin that gave us the real scare.

When we were out catching snakes for our display, we saw a large cottonmouth water moccasin, a snake that can deliver a deadly bite. Even when its bite is not

16

deadly, it can keep you in the hospital for weeks. We had one snake stick between us. (A snake stick is a metal pole with an L-shaped end which is used to hold the snake's head to the ground.) I tossed the stick to Bill, and he set off after the cottonmouth. Bill caught up with the snake and got the snake stick under it just as it was about to vanish into the swamp. Bill gave a mighty heave, sending the snake back over his shoulder. Unfortunately, the snake landed on me, hitting me in the chest, then falling to the ground with a thud. Luckily, I jumped back before the startled snake could strike. I believe that was the fastest I have ever moved. I did not get bitten, although neither Bill nor I can take credit for that fact. We were acting irresponsibly around a dangerous wild animal, and I almost paid a very high price. If the cottonmouth had bitten me, I could have died.

For a long time after that, I would wake up in the middle of the night gasping for breath as I relived the episode in my dreams. The skunk in Methuen had gotten me; the cottonmouth water moccasin in Louisiana had not. I learned a very important lesson: It is easy to be too sure of yourself around wild animals, but this can get you into trouble. I have never been careless around venomous snakes since. And I vowed to be much more careful around all wild animals in the future.

We had a display of dangerous black widow spiders and a cage with a very impressive hairy tarantula. The little black widow spider can actually kill a grown man, but the giant tarantula gives a jab no worse than a bee sting. I knew that for a fact because I got jabbed when I captured it.

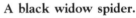

A black widow spider.

Penguins: The Tip of the Iceberg

Roger and Jill in 1954.

Antarctica is the coldest continent on earth. During winter months it remains dark twenty-four hours a day. Antarctica holds ninety percent of the world's ice, and in some places this ice can be more than two miles thick!

The army took me to Germany, California, Hawaii, Japan, Korea, the Philippines, and Guam. After finishing my time with the army, I went to college and studied natural history, filmmaking, and writing. I graduated from the University of Southern California in 1954 with a degree in cinema. Shortly thereafter, I met a lovely young girl named Jill Barclay, who had the same interests as I had. In time she became my wife.

During my travels with the army, and later in college, I continued writing about nature. I made notes, kept diaries, and eventually sold articles to magazines and newspapers. I also read everything on nature I could find. As I became known as a nature writer, requests came to appear on radio and television shows. A career was building, and life was becoming very exciting. But soon it was to get even more so.

In 1961 I was living in New York City and working at Columbia Pictures as a press agent. I also produced a record album of the nuclear submarine *Nautilus*'s trip to the North Pole. (It recorded all of the ship's sounds and voices of the crew members on their journey.) Because of this and my experience in the army, I was asked if I would like to be a guest of an American scientific expedition in the South Pole, which is located in Antarctica. *Would I like to visit the Antarctic?* I had never said "yes" to anything so fast in my life. All I had to do in return was write and broadcast a story about the navy's part in the scientific exploration. I could write about seals, whales, penguins, the weather, snow, ice—anything at all.

Exploring the South Pole was like experiencing a whole new world. Temperatures there can drop to 100 degrees below zero and the winds can reach almost 200 miles an hour. (I had my cameras specially treated so they wouldn't freeze up.) The base where I was staying, McMurdo Sound, is on the edge of the Ross Sea, and sits beneath the world's southernmost active volcano, Mount Erebus, which is over 12,000 feet high.

One of the first things I realized about Antarctica was that there aren't many land animals there. In fact, one of the largest is a wingless mosquito! There are no people, aside from scientific explorers, and there are no polar bears (they live at the opposite end of the earth, in the Arctic). But there is a variety of sea animals:

McMurdo Sound, the base where Roger stayed during his trip to Antarctica.

An Adelie penguin rookery. In some rookeries there can be almost a million birds.

penguins, seals, and whales. Somehow it was penguins that most captured my attention.

Penguins nest in very large colonies called *rookeries*, and there can be millions of birds living in them. Getting to the remote rookeries, however, can be a problem. The only practical way to make the journey there is by helicopter.

Cape Royds is the Adelie penguin rookery closest to McMurdo Sound and is located where ice from the Ross Sea meets ice from the Antarctic continent. This meeting creates massive formations of ice and snow. The sea ice and land ice butt against each other, buckling upward, creating towers of ice, called *pressure ridges*. Travel is slow and extremely uncomfortable. It is also dangerous because of the possibility of slipping down steep slopes of ice and vanishing into crevasses.

I waited several days for a helicopter that was going in the direction of the Cape Royds rookery. When it finally came, I was in my hut. A young naval officer opened my door, stuck his head in, and told me I had ten minutes to get ready.

Paddling around in my stocking feet, I rushed to get ready, and in so doing kicked the steel leg of a table. I leapt around on one foot, moaning loudly, as I got my cameras and a tape recorder organized. Then I had to put my boots on. Tugging the heavy boot on over my injured foot was more painful than almost anything I have ever felt. (I later found out that I had broken three toes!)

I hobbled out to the helicopter with my foot

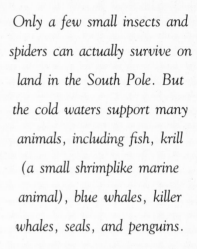

Only a few small insects and spiders can actually survive on land in the South Pole. But the cold waters support many animals, including fish, krill (a small shrimplike marine animal), blue whales, killer whales, seals, and penguins.

Adelie penguins diving into the cold ocean.

Since there are no predators on "land" in the Antarctic, penguins don't have a sense of fear when they are out of the water. But the Antarctic waters can be very dangerous. Killer whales and leopard seals both prey on penguins.

throbbing as if it would explode inside my boot. Then we took off, and in half an hour we settled down about a mile from the rookery. Helicopters aren't allowed to get any closer than that because they might frighten the birds off their eggs and away from their young. Carrying two cameras, a long telephoto lens, and a tape recorder, I had to crawl on my hands and knees for a mile over the jagged ice, wondering every minute if the snow would hold beneath me. I was numb from lack of sleep, and it was about seventy degrees below zero. Cold, tired, and in pain, I wondered why I was there. But as I slithered up over the last icy ridge, I saw the rookery spread out before me and I knew why. There were hundreds of thousands of penguins. The sight was amazing—a huge sea of little black-and-white birds. And the sound!

It is a sound very hard to describe, but it sounds more like a noise that might be made in a factory full of power tools than by some small birds.

I was able to crawl down to the rookery and walk among the sea of penguins. The birds were not concerned about me, the lumbering giant in their midst. They tried to peck the laces out of my boots and pulled on my woolen pants. As I walked among these fascinating birds, I realized how much I had learned about penguins by watching and hearing them in their natural habitat. In fact, it was during this Antarctica trip that I started my practice of writing about an animal only after observing it in its own environment first.

Two penguins perform the nesting ritual.

I observed these exotic penguins for days. I learned that, because there are no trees in Antarctica, they don't build nests with sticks or branches. They have to be a bit more creative. They push a few pebbles together and lay a single egg among them. When a male finds a rare pebble, he takes it to a female and places it at her feet. If she walks away, he picks the pebble up and waddles around in search of another mate. If a female *looks* at the pebble, the male gets very excited—and noisy. If the female pushes the pebble around with her beak and then picks it up, the male goes wild, for that means he has found his mate. The two birds then

Both the male and female Adelie penguins care for their eggs and chicks.

stand facing each other with their beaks pointed toward the sky. They screech and chirp at the same time.

It is while the couple is serenading each other that trouble can begin. Another male, who also wants to make a nest, will sneak up and steal the precious bit of stone from the new couple. The male who has been robbed of the pebble then sets off after the thief and beats him with his stubby wings and beak in an effort to get his pebble back. A crowd of penguins in the area stop what they are doing—which is usually stealing pebbles themselves—and start screeching as if to cheer on the victim. This fighting between penguins is quite common during mating season.

Broken toes and all, this trip to Cape Royds turned out to be one of the most fascinating trips of my life, and an experience which influenced my work from then on. When I got back from Antarctica, I had enough material for my first book. A year later, *Antarctica: Land of Frozen Time* was published. I then began to appear on radio and television shows regularly, including the "Today" show (where I became their "house" naturalist for eight years). What started as adventurous traveling was becoming a livelihood. This emerging career took me to the most exotic places, but one place I still longed to see was Africa. Little did I know I would soon have my chance.

Penguins swim in the frigid Antarctic waters.

Penguins are more at home in the sea than on land. In water they can propel themselves very quickly using their wings as flippers. Penguins usually only come to land to breed, and the rest of the time they spend entirely at sea.

AFRICA: MY DREAM COME TRUE

Africa is home to a wide variety of animals.

Africa is the second largest continent in the world. It is more than three times the size of the United States, and in fact, it is larger than the United States, Europe, and China combined!

Africa was the one place I had always longed to travel. I often imagined what Africa would look like—vast, pristine landscapes filled with exotic, wild animals. I wanted to go to beautiful places like India, the South Pacific, and Alaska, and in time I would do so, but Africa was the place I most wanted to see with my own eyes. And so a phone call from Columbia Pictures with an invitation to go to Africa was one of the most exciting calls I have ever received.

In 1971 Columbia Pictures was making a second motion picture about George and Joy Adamson, two world-famous naturalists. Called *Living Free*, it would be the sequel to the first film (called *Born Free*) about the Adamsons' adventures with Elsa, an orphan lion cub whom they raised and later set free. Since I had worked for Columbia Pictures in the past and I was friends with Joy Adamson, I was asked to write and direct a documentary film about the making of the second movie. Jill and I sat up half the night talking about it. I think we were secretly pinching ourselves to be sure we weren't dreaming.

Jill Caras and Joy Adamson sightseeing.

A month later we flew into Nairobi, Kenya, where we began the sixty-five-mile trip into the Great Rift Valley, and then on to beautiful Lake Naivasha, where

A group of giraffes.

Standing up to 19 and 1/2 feet tall, the giraffe is the tallest land animal. Its long legs and neck allow it to reach leaves and branches that are out of reach to other animals. Giraffes usually live in troops of six to twelve animals, consisting of one male, several females, and young.

This apparent yawn is really a threat display warning others to stay away.

Hippos spend their days resting in water. At night they emerge to feed on grass, plants, and fruit. Hippos live in groups called pods. Males fiercely defend members of the pod and their territory. To threaten a rival, a male hippo opens his huge mouth, exposing his big teeth, and bellows.

Joy Adamson lived. On our way to Lake Naivasha, we came to a traffic jam. A group of seventeen giraffes was feeding along the road, completely ignoring cars, trucks, and buses. It seemed as if we would be there forever, but the jam came to an end when a young boy peddled by on his bicycle. He whistled at the giraffes, and they quickly vanished into the trees beside the road. Jill and I both knew that we had come to a very special place.

Although this was a working trip, once we got there we had a lot of free time to explore. We traveled with Joy and began learning about the Africa she knew and loved so much. Joy took us to an area called Samburu National Park in northern Kenya. It is filled with fantastic wildlife of many kinds: cheetahs, lions, leopards, zebras, giraffes, antelope, and a dazzling array of birds. It is a naturalist's wonderland.

Tourists from all over the world come to this park to watch the wild animals within their own habitat. Every afternoon at the park the people who operate the tourist lodges put meat scraps out along the riverbank to attract crocodiles. Stone walls and iron spikes keep the crocodiles and tourists from mingling. (Crocodiles are carnivores, and they eat any animal they can overpower and pull underwater, so no one would want to get too close.) Eventually the crocodiles smell the meat, and their V-shaped wakes appear on the river's surface as they swim toward shore for food. It looks as if a hidden force is pushing large logs through the water. Then the crocodiles haul themselves onto the riverbank. The big crocodiles shoulder aside the smaller ones and begin their feast. Amazingly, small African wildcats, not much larger than house cats, appear alongside the crocodiles. Fierce little spotted genet cats, which are not really cats at all but a kind of mongoose, also appear. The genets and wildcats dash in among the huge crocodiles, snatching away scraps of meat for themselves. They put themselves in danger each time—any bad timing, and they would be gone.

Though the wildcats and genets are skillful and daring, many animals in the wild aren't so lucky. Once, I

The Nile crocodile lives in rivers, lakes, and marshes. Young crocodiles eat fish and insects, but when they grow larger, they prey upon birds and mammals that come to the water to drink. The crocodile snatches its prey from the water's edge and drowns it before beginning to eat.

Crocodiles spend a lot of time sunning themselves.

A lioness feeds with her cubs.

saw a pride of lions feeding on a magnificent giraffe bull. The lions had blood all over their faces and paws, and they were cleaning themselves by licking each other and their cubs. These lions were full and content, but the handsome giraffe was dead. Watching this scene made me realize that one of the toughest challenges of being a naturalist is to accept that some animals must die so that others can live. It is difficult not to take sides when you love all kinds of animals. But anyone who appreciates the natural world must come to terms with this dilemma. So I chose to study the world of animals by simply being an observer, without choosing sides or interfering. It's not always easy being an observer, but interfering or choosing sides would mean upsetting the balance of the natural world—the world I love and strive to preserve.

An elephant mother and her baby. Female elephants are very good mothers.

THE ROYAL TUSKER OF SRI LANKA

The lush jungle of Sri Lanka is home to many animals.

Sri Lanka (Sree-lon-ka) is an island in the Indian Ocean, off the southeast tip of India. Its indigenous peoples, mostly Sinhalese and Tamils, gained their independence from British rule in 1948.

Sri Lanka is an island in the Indian Ocean, southeast of India. The jungles and forests there are home to elephants, sambars (a kind of deer), water buffaloes, mugger crocodiles, leopards, Asian black bears, pythons, cobras, great monitor lizards, and many birds. In 1981 I traveled to Sri Lanka to do a report on the vanishing indigenous, or native, people of this area. (Like many animal species, some human cultures are disappearing because their homelands are being used up or destroyed.)

While conducting my research in Sri Lanka, I heard rumors about a huge male elephant with giant tusks.

This was exciting because Asian elephants seldom have tusks as big as the larger African elephant, and an Asian elephant so equipped is often referred to as a *koomeriah*, or "royal tusker." Because they are so rare, it is quite exciting when one shows up.

As reports of this giant elephant increased in number, I decided try to see it for myself. The elephant had been sighted walking along the beach in Ruhunu National Park, in the southeast part of the country. It was thought to be at least thirty years old, and the mystery was, where had he been living all this time? It was believed that he must have come from the mountains beyond the park boundaries.

I asked a friend named Thambi, who was also a naturalist and a native of Sri Lanka, to be my guide. Thambi and I headed toward the southern coast and found that we were not the only ones who wanted to see and photograph the *koomeriah*. The Sri Lankan Tourist Department had sent a jeep of photographers, and several news organizations were there as well. Day after day we all crisscrossed the park. We stopped frequently and compared notes on which areas had been covered and how recently. One by one the photographers gave up, claiming that the *koomeriah* was just another local legend. By the end of one week only the tourist office photographers and Thambi

Wild water buffalo.

Sambar deer are native to Sri Lanka.

and myself remained. Convinced it was just a hoax, the tourist office team gave up, but Thambi and I decided to continue the search for another twenty-four hours.

Not more than several minutes after the other photographers left, we came around a clump of trees and looked out across a lake. A group of elephants had stepped out of the heavy forest and into the water. Among them was the great *koomeriah*.

His tusks were enormous—probably weighing over one hundred and fifty pounds each! They curved down in great arcs and ended with the points nearly touching each other.

The royal tusker stayed in the water, mingling with the rest of the herd for almost an hour. Because of our patience and persistence, we had a rare and wonderful opportunity to watch the group interact. The elephants treated him no differently than they did any other member of the herd. To us he was a living legend, but to the elephants he lived with, he was just another elephant.

When we got back to Colombo (the captial of Sri Lanka), several of the others who had tried to see the royal tusker wanted to hear about him. We all agreed that it was luck, but also patience, that had allowed Thambi and me to see the *koomeriah*.

Having the opportunity to observe such a rare animal taught me that patience is a naturalist's best friend. An animal does not appear before you just because you're waiting for it. It takes time, patience, and luck. That old *koomeriah* with its long, majestic tusks tested my patience to the limit. But all my waiting—and frustration—was rewarded with a wonderful experience.

It's easy to pick out the *koomeriah* among the elephant herd.

SAVING THE ANIMALS

As president of the ASPCA, Roger is the voice for millions of animals. Here Roger speaks to Congress about the Animal Welfare Act.

From Antarctica to Sri Lanka, I have seen some of the world's most fascinating wildlife. But there are many animals in our own country that need attention, too. So after my many years of traveling, talking, and writing about animals, I decided to help them more directly. In 1991 I was named president of the ASPCA.

The ASPCA is the oldest humane society in America, founded in 1866, and is one of the largest in the world. The society's main goal is to prevent cruelty to animals. As its president, I direct the organization in its efforts to provide "hands-on" services, like medical treatment and shelter for injured and abandoned animals; legislation and enforcement that help animals throughout the United States and the world; and education programs for children and adults.

The "hands-on" care of sick and abandoned animals is probably the ASPCA's most well-known responsibility. When people call us and tell us that an animal is hurt, we try to get it out of the hurtful environment and give it proper medical treatment. When animals are sick, they can come to our hospitals for care. When people can't keep animals anymore or an abandoned animal is found, it can be brought to us and we try to find it a new home. Luckily, we do find homes for thousands of animals.

The ASPCA also works with the government to pass laws that ensure people are kind to animals. We also want to strengthen the Animal Welfare Act—a bill of rights for animals—to include strict laws for the kind treatment of animals in entertainment.

Henry Bergh, founder of the ASPCA, stated the organization's main goal: "To provide effective means for the prevention of cruelty to animals throughout the United States." In 1866 the New York state legislature made it a crime to be cruel to animals.

The laws we have worked so hard to pass also have to be enforced. The ASPCA has a Humane Law Enforcement Department, which investigates cases of animal cruelty. For example, once someone called and told us about a man who had been in South America for at least a month and had left his exotic birds in his locked-up apartment. So the ASPCA got a warrant to go inside his apartment.´ The home was filled with rare, exotic birds: cockatoos, macaws, and parrots. They didn't have any food

Roger and the ASPCA work to make and enforce laws that protect animals in entertainment.

or water. They had been captured in the wild and brought to the United States and locked up in this man's home. We took all of the birds to our hospital. These birds were then sent to zoos and specialists who knew how to care for them. Fortunately, U.S. customs officials shortly thereafter arrested the man who had left the birds.

The ASPCA also has educational programs about domestic animal welfare. People need to learn how they can provide responsible care for pets, and so we try to teach them how to do this. Too many puppies and kittens are born, and there are not enough homes available for them, and animal shelters can't house them all. The

With the help of the ASPCA, these stray kittens have found new homes.

37

sad result is that over ten million dogs and cats in the United States have to be put to sleep every single year. To avoid this overpopulation, dogs and cats can be spayed and neutered (simple operations that will keep them from having unwanted puppies and kittens). In addition, we try to encourage people to adopt from local shelters.

At the ASPCA I have used my experience to teach and promote humanitarian treatment of animals. I have spent my life caring deeply about animals, and I love being able to do something to help them. Other people who work for the ASPCA have a passion for animals, too, but they aren't necessarily journalists—like myself—or even scientists. They are veterinarians, teachers, and volunteers who all care deeply enough to try and make the world a happier and healthier place for animals. From grand lions in Africa to pet kittens at home, all animals deserve our respect and require our help.

The ASPCA visits schools throughout the country, teaching children how to provide proper care for pets.

The ASPCA promotes kind treatment to domestic animals, as well as exotic
animals that are brought into the United States.

Afterword

Many people love animals, but you wouldn't know it by the way we treat them. Around the world, pollution and habitat destruction have taken their toll on animal life. Unless habitats are preserved and kept clean, and unless we leave large areas of land undisturbed, many of the world's animals will become extinct. Cruel treatment of animals has also had its deadly effects. Millions of animals are mistreated or abandoned, and ultimately die because of our lack of understanding and care.

But is not too late to help. There is much you can do. Many young people's groups are doing important work for our world, and it is possible to get involved wherever you are and whatever your interests may be. You can volunteer to work for a zoo, a museum, a humane society, or an animal shelter. You can join school environmental clubs and other youth groups that help protect the environment. Whatever your interests—rocks and minerals, mammals, insects, fish, birds, reptiles, plants, weather, the ocean, or any other part of the environment—you can find books that will tell you more about that subject. You may want to travel, to see things on your own, but a trip need not be to some faraway place. You can go into a park or your own backyard, lie on your stomach, and spread the grass with your hands. That, too, is a trip into the natural world. And if you know what to look for, what you can find there is amazing.

As a child, I found it very exciting that our world was full of animals. As I grew up, I wanted to help convince people to keep it that way, and I wanted to help improve the lives of all animals. Devoting my life to animals was the best decision I ever made. I wouldn't dream of doing anything else. And you can become a naturalist, too, no matter what your interests and talents may be. If we all become naturalists in one way or another, and if we all strive to understand and preserve nature, the world just might stay full of animals.

Organizations

There are many organizations working to protect and preserve wildlife. If you would like to become a member, if you would like to help, or if you would like more information, you can contact any one of the following groups:

ASPCA
424 East 92nd Street
New York, NY 10128
(212) 876-7700

Greenpeace U.S.A.
1432 U Street, N.W.
Washington, DC 20009
(202) 462-1177

National Wildlife Foundation
1400 16th Street, N.W.
Washington, DC 20036
(202) 797-6800

Nature Conservancy
1815 North Lynn Street
Arlington, VA 22209
(703) 841-5300

The Wildlife Conservation Society
The International Conservation Park
Bronx, NY 10460
(718) 220-5155

World Wildlife Fund
1250 24th Street, N.W.
Washington, DC 20037
(202) 293-4800

Glossary

Abandon: To leave without meaning to return.

Animal shelter: A place that offers protection and help for animals.

Animal Welfare Act: The law that protects all types of animals from cruel treatment.

Antarctica: The area surrounding and including the South Pole, the southernmost point of the earth.

Arctic: The area surrounding and including the North Pole, the northernmost point of the earth.

Breed: To produce offspring, or young.

Carnivore: A meat-eating animal.

Colony: A group of one animal species living together in a particular area.

Correspondent: A journalist who travels to different locations and reports information on television, radio, or in newspapers and magazines.

Domestic animal: Any animal that lives and breeds in a human environment, e.g., a dog or a cat.

Environment: The natural surroundings of a particular area.

Expedition: A journey or trip with a specific purpose.

Extinct: No longer in existence.

Habitat: A place where groups of plants and animals naturally live and grow.

Herd: Any large number of animals which live and travel together.

Humanitarian: A person concerned with human and animal welfare.

Indigenous: Being native to a geographic area.

Legislation: The making of laws.

Mammal: Any warm-blooded animal usually having hair covering its skin. Hair can be fur, wool, quills, and even certain horns. Mammal mothers give birth to live young and feed them with milk from mammary glands.

Mate: A male or female member of a breeding pair of animals.

Mating season: The time of year when animals breed.

Natural history: The study of the natural world, including animals and plants.

Naturalist: A person who studies the natural world, such as plants, animals, or environments.

Nest: A place prepared by an animal for its eggs and young.

Nocturnal: Active at night.

Pod: A group of animals clustered together, such as whales, seals, and hippos.

Predator: An animal that hunts and eats other animals.

Prey: An animal that is hunted and eaten by other animals.

Pride: A group of lions.

Rookery: A breeding place for birds such as penguins.

Territory: An area that is occupied and defended by an animal or group of animals.

Threat display: An action or sign given by an animal as a warning for other animals to stay away.

Venomous: Poisonous.

Veterinarian: A doctor who treats animals.

INDEX

abandoned animal, 36, 40
ABC News, 8
Adamson, George, 26, 27
Adamson, Joy, 26, 27, 28
Adelie, 21–25
Africa, 8, 9, 11, 25–28, 39
African elephant, 33, 34
African wildcat, 29
Angell Memorial Animal
    Hospital, 15
animal cruelty, 36, 37, 40
animal shelter, 36, 37, 38, 41
Animal Welfare Act, 36
animal welfare, 9, 36
Antarctica, 18–25, 36
Antarctic: Land of Frozen Time, 25
Arctic, 19
army, 15, 18
Asian elephant, 32, 33, 34
ASPCA, 9, 36–39
Bergh, Henry, 36
bird, 11, 21, 22–25, 28, 32, 37, 41
Born Free, 27
Boston, 11, 15
Bozo (dog), 12
camera, 19, 21, 22
Cape Royds, 21–24, 25
Camp Polk, 15, 16
Caras,
    Bessie (mother), 11, 12, 13
    Jill Barclay, 9, 18, 27, 28
    Joseph (father), 11
    Marshall, 11
    Sheldon, 11, 12
carnivore, 28
cat, 9, 12, 15, 29, 37, 58
China, 8, 11, 26
Columbia Pictures, 18, 26, 27
Colombo, 35
congress, 36
cottonmouth water moccasin,
    16, 17
crocodile, 28, 29
Darwin, Charles, 15
deer, 11, 16, 32
documentary, 27
dog, 9, 11, 15, 37, 38

domestic animal, 37
egg, 22, 24
egg case, (*ootheca*), 12
Elsa (lion), 27
environment, 8, 23, 41
extinct, 40
Exxon Valdez, 8–9
fish, 17, 21, 29, 41
genet cat, 29
giraffe, 28, 30
glacier, 21
Great Rift Valley, 27
habitat, 8, 9, 40
hippopotamus, 28
Humane Law Enforcement
    Department, 37
humane society, 36, 40
India, 26, 32
Indian Ocean, 32
indigenous, 32
insect, 11, 16, 21, 29, 41
journalist, 8, 39
Kenya, 27, 28
killer whale, 21, 22
koomeriah, 33–35
Lake Naivasha, 27, 28
leopard, 28, 32
lion, 27, 28, 30
Living Free, 27
Louisiana, 15, 17
McMurdo Sound, 19, 21
Maryland, 9
Massachusetts, 15
mate, 24, 25
Methuen, 11, 13, 17
mosquito, 11, 19
Mount Erebus, 19
Nairobi, 27
naturalist, 8, 9, 25, 27, 28,
    30, 33, 35, 41
Nautilus, 18
navy, 19
nest, 11, 24, 25
network correspondent, 8
New York City, 18
newspaper, 8, 18
Nile crocodile, 29

North Pole, 18
penguin, 19, 21–25
pet, 12, 37, 38
Peter (dog), 12, 15
photographer, 8, 33
polar bear, 19
pollution, 40
praying mantis, 12
predator, 22
pressure ridge, 21
prey, 22, 29
Pryor, Bill, 16, 17
radio, 9, 18, 25
rookery, 21, 22, 23
royal tusker, 33–35
Ross Sea, 19
Ruhunu National Park, 33
sambar, 32
Samburu National Park, 28
scientist, 39
seal, 19, 21
skunk, 12, 13, 17
snake, 11, 16, 17
snake stick, 16
South America, 9, 37
South Pole, 18, 19
spay (neuter), 38
spider, black widow, 16
Spickett River, 11, 13
Sri Lanka, 8, 32, 33, 35, 36
television, 8, 9, 18, 25
territory, 28
Thambi, 33, 34, 35
Thistle Hill, 9
threat display, 28
"Today" show, 25
tusks, 32, 34
United States, 9, 26, 36, 37, 38
veterinarian, 38
volunteer, 38, 40
Voyage of the Beagle, The, 15
water buffalo, domestic, 33
water buffalo, wild, 33
youth group, 41
zoo, 37, 41

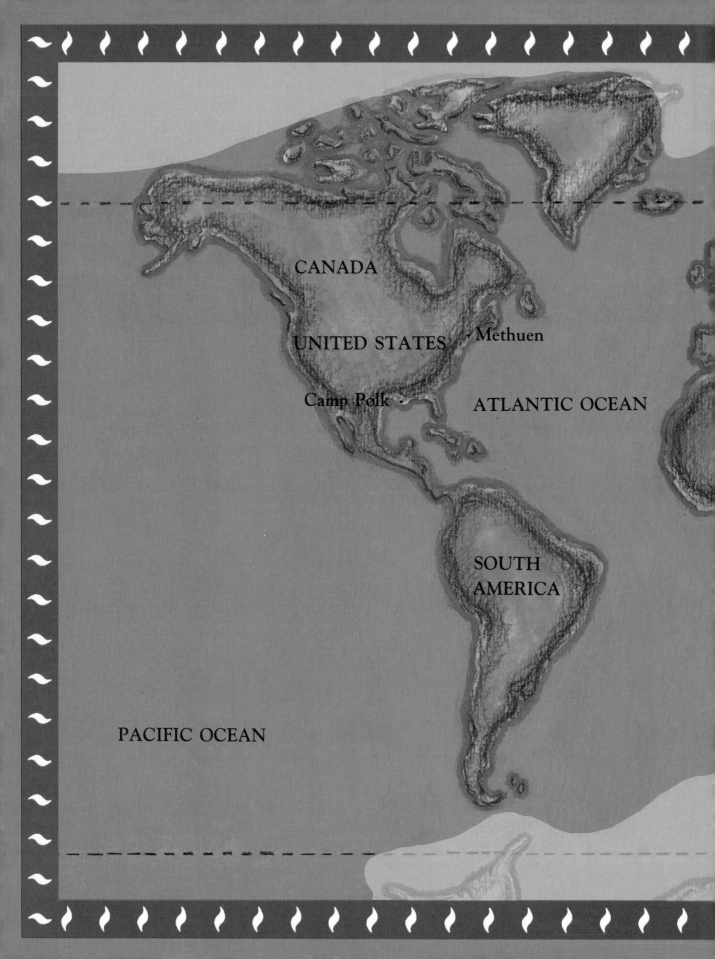

J
B
CARAS

Caras, Roger A.

A world full of animals.